TDD IN PRACTICE
WITH ELIXIR

A Learning Journey Through Test-Driven Development with Elixir

Guilherme Ferreira

This book is dedicated to my family, the pillar of my life, which provides me with unconditional support at every step I take. To my wife, Aline, who shares with me the joys and challenges of our journey, offering unparalleled love, understanding, and partnership. To my son, Murilo, whose smile and curiosity about the world inspire me every day to be the best version of myself.

I extend this dedication to my relatives and friends, whose support, encouragement, and presence have been fundamental in my personal and professional trajectory. You are the stars that illuminate my path, providing joy and comfort in moments of doubt and uncertainty.

To my colleagues at work, whose collaboration, innovation, and commitment not only enrich our professional environment but also shape the future of technology. Together, we face challenges, celebrate achievements, and continue to learn from each other every day.

Last but not least, I thank my students spread throughout Brazil and the world. You are the reason why I dedicate myself to teaching and sharing knowledge. Seeing the growth and success of each one of you is the greatest reward an educator can receive. This book is also for you, in the hope that it can light your way in the world of software development and beyond.

CONTENTS

PROLOGUE

Before we dive into the depths of Test-Driven Development (TDD) and discover the wonders of programming with Elixir, I invite you to pause and contemplate the beginning of an extraordinary journey. This is not just a book about writing tests or using a programming language; it is an adventure that will transform the way you think and approach software creation.

Imagine yourself as a craftsman, where each line of code is a brushstroke on your masterpiece. TDD and Elixir are your tools, but the true magic lies in your ability to combine them to create something lasting and beautiful. We are about to embark on a journey that challenges conventions, embraces experimentation, and celebrates continuous learning.

Get ready to explore new territories, overcome obstacles, and discover the deep satisfaction that comes from building robust, elegant, and functional software. Welcome to a world where quality leads development, and a passion for programming is the compass that guides us.

PREFACE

As I embarked on the journey of writing this book, I reflected deeply on the many hours I spent in front of my computer, hands on the keyboard, immersed in the universe of Test-Driven Development (TDD) with Elixir. It's not just a software development practice to me; it has become a philosophy, a way to face challenges and solve them with precision and confidence.

The satisfaction of writing code using TDD with Elixir is something hard to put into words, but it's an experience that has profoundly transformed the way I develop software. Each function, each module that emerges from the red-green-refactor cycle is not just a piece of code; it's a carefully tested and validated piece of a larger puzzle. Elixir, with its elegant concurrency and robust features, provides the perfect environment for this meticulous approach.

I vividly remember the first times I applied TDD in real projects, feeling a mix of anxiety and excitement. The anxiety came from the fear of the unknown, the concern of spending too much time on tests instead of "really coding." However, this perception changed quickly as the benefits became clear. The excitement, on the other hand, stemmed from discovering a new way of working, one that elevated the quality of my code to levels I hadn't imagined possible.

The true reward of adopting TDD with Elixir manifested at the moment of task delivery. The act of delivering a complex functionality, knowing that it had been meticulously tested, without having to spend hours or days fixing bugs after the release, is immensely gratifying. The absence of bugs and the quality of the delivery are not just proof of the effort and attention to detail invested but also a testimony to the effectiveness of TDD.

This methodology has taught me to value prevention over correction, to plan before acting, and to appreciate the beauty of well-written and well-tested code. It has become second nature to approach each new feature with the mindset that if it's worth doing, it's worth being well tested.

Writing this book was an opportunity to share that passion and the knowledge gained over the years. It was a journey of reflection on my own practices and a chance to engage with other developers who, perhaps, are seeking ways to improve the quality and efficiency of their work.

My wish is that by sharing my experience with TDD and Elixir, I can inspire other developers to adopt this approach, experience the same satisfaction and pride in their work, and discover the profound impact that a dedication to detail and quality can have on their careers and the software industry as a whole.

INTRODUCTION TO ELIXIR

What is Elixir?

Elixir is a dynamic, functional programming language created by José Valim, aimed at the development of scalable and easily maintainable applications. It is based on the Erlang Virtual Machine (BEAM), which is renowned for running highly available distributed systems.

Key Features

Concurrency

Concurrency in Elixir is managed by Erlang's actor model, where lightweight processes communicate through message passing. This model facilitates the development of applications that perform multiple tasks simultaneously in an effective manner.

Practical Example:
Imagine you want to create simultaneous processes to perform independent tasks. In Elixir, you can easily start processes and send messages between them:

```
my_project > lib >  example.ex > ...
1    defmodule Example do
2      def send_message(pid) do
3        send(pid, {:hello, "from Elixir"})
4      end
5
6      def receive_message do
7        receive do
8          {:hello, msg} -> IO.puts(msg)
9        end
10     end
11   end
12
13   pid = spawn(Example, :receive_message, [])
14   Example.send_message(pid)
15
```

To run, simply use the terminal and execute: elixir example.ex

This code demonstrates the creation of a process that waits to receive a message and a second process that sends a message to the first. The communication is done asynchronously and in isolation.

Fault Tolerance

Elixir uses supervisors to ensure system resilience. Supervisors monitor child processes and apply restart strategies in case of failures, promoting high availability.

Metaprogramming

Elixir allows metaprogramming with macros, which are code expansions at compile time, making it easier to create DSLs (Domain-Specific Languages) and reducing repetition.

Immutability

All data in Elixir are immutable, which simplifies reasoning about the program state and increases the security of applications.

Elegant Syntax

Elixir offers a clear and modern syntax, making code reading and writing easier, as well as promoting a pleasant development experience.

WHY IS ELIXIR A GOOD CHOICE FOR TDD?

Facilitated Testing

T he immutability and functional style of Elixir make functions easier to test. Each function can be tested in isolation, ensuring that it produces the same result for the same inputs.

Test Example with ExUnit:

Let's write a simple test using ExUnit, the test framework that comes with Elixir:

```
my_project > test > 🍵 math_test.exs > ...
  1  defmodule MathTest do
  2    use ExUnit.Case
  3
  4    test "sum of two numbers" do
  5      assert 2 + 3 == 5
  6    end
  7  end
  8
```

This example shows a basic test verifying the sum of two numbers, demonstrating the simplicity of writing and running tests in Elixir.

Quick Feedback Loop

The quick feedback loop is essential in TDD, and Elixir, with tools like Mix, makes this process easier. Mix allows you to compile the project, run tests, manage dependencies, and much more with ease.

Elixir is a robust choice for developers seeking a modern and functional language that offers integrated tools for testing and test-driven development (TDD). The language encourages clean and safe code practices, while the Elixir ecosystem supports agile and efficient development.

FUNDAMENTALS
OF TDD

T est-Driven Development (TDD) is a software development methodology that emphasizes writing automated tests before the production code. The TDD process can be summarized in a simple cycle: Red-Green-Refactor.

Red-Green-Refactor Cycle

Red

You start by writing a test for a new feature that has not yet been implemented. Since the corresponding code for the feature does not exist, the test will fail. This state is called "Red" because, in many testing tools, failures are indicated by the color red.

Example:
Suppose we want to develop a function that calculates the sum of two numbers. First, we write the test:

```
my_project > test > 🔥 math_test.exs > ...
▷   1   defmodule MathTest do
    2     use ExUnit.Case
    3
▷   4     test "sum of 1 and 2 equals 3" do
    5       assert Math.sum(1, 2) == 3
    6     end
    7   end
    8
```

Since the function Math.sum/2 has not yet been implemented, this test will fail if you try to run it.

Green

The next step is to write the minimum amount of code necessary to make the test pass. The goal is simply to get a "Green" test, meaning a successful test.
Example:
Here is the simplest implementation that makes the previous test pass:

```
my_project > lib > 🔥 math.ex > ...
    1   defmodule Math do
    2     def sum(a, b) do
    3       a + b
    4     end
    5   end
    6
```

Running the test now, it will pass, indicating success with the color green.

Refactor

With the test passing, you can refactor the code, improving its structure, design, or efficiency without changing its behavior. After refactoring, the tests should be run again to ensure that no functionality has been broken.

Example:
Suppose that, in the broader context of the project, you realize that the sum function will often be called with lists of numbers. You can refactor the code to accept a list of numbers, improving flexibility:

my_project > lib > 🔥 math.ex > ...

```
1   defmodule Math do
2     def sum(numbers) when is_list(numbers) do
3       Enum.reduce(numbers, 0, &(&1 + &2))
4     end
5   end
6
```

And update the corresponding test:

my_project > test > 🔥 math_test.exs > ...

```
1   defmodule MathTest do
2     use ExUnit.Case
3
4     test "sum of a list of numbers" do
5       assert Math.sum([1, 2]) == 3
6     end
7   end
8
```

Importance of Automated Testing

Automated tests are essential in TDD because they provide a safety net that allows developers to modify and refactor code with confidence, ensuring that existing functionalities remain intact.

Benefits of TDD

Improved Code Quality: TDD helps to identify issues early in the development cycle, reducing bugs.

Enhanced Software Design: By writing tests first, developers are forced to think about the interface and design of the code, resulting in cleaner and more modular systems.

Living Documentation

Tests provide up-to-date documentation of how the system is supposed to behave.

Agile Development

TDD encourages small iterations of improvements, which aligns well with agile methodologies.

SETTING UP THE ELIXIR DEVELOPMENT ENVIRONMENT FOR TDD

Before starting the practice of Test-Driven Development (TDD) with Elixir, it is essential to properly set up the development environment. This includes installing Elixir and becoming familiar with essential tools like Mix and ExUnit.

Elixir Installation

To ensure that you have the most up-to-date and effective instructions for installing Elixir, we recommend following the guidance provided on the official Elixir website. The installation process can vary depending on your operating system (Windows, macOS, Linux), and the official site offers detailed guides for each platform.

Visit elixir-lang.org for detailed instructions on how to install Elixir on your machine.

After installation, you can verify that Elixir has been installed correctly by running elixir -v in your terminal. This should display the Elixir version, confirming that the installation was successful.

Setting Up an Elixir Project with Mix

Mix is a build tool that comes with Elixir, making it easy to create projects, manage tasks, dependencies, and much more.

To start a new Elixir project with Mix, execute the following command in the terminal:

```
mix new my_project --module MyProject
```

This will create a new directory called my_project with a standard Elixir project structure, including a lib directory for your code and a test directory for your tests, as well as a mix.exs file that defines your project and its dependencies.

ExUnit for Testing

ExUnit is the testing framework built into Elixir, ready for use as soon as you create a new project with Mix. Within your project's test directory, you can begin writing your tests.

Example of a Simple Test with ExUnit:

To test a function that returns "Hello, world!", you would write:

my_project/lib/my_project.ex:

my_project > lib > 🍂 my_project.ex > ...

```elixir
 1  defmodule MyProject do
 2    @moduledoc """
 3    Documentation for `MyProject`.
 4    """
 5
 6    @doc """
 7    Hello world.
 8
 9    ## Examples
10
11        iex> MyProject.hello()
12        :world
13
14    """
15    def hello do
16      :world
17    end
18  end
19
```

my_project/test/my_project_test.exs:

my_project > test > 🍂 my_project_test.exs > ...

```elixir
 1  defmodule MyProjectTest do
 2    use ExUnit.Case
 3    doctest MyProject
 4
 5    test "greets the world" do
 6      assert MyProject.hello() == :world
 7    end
 8  end
 9
```

To run your tests, navigate to your project directory in the terminal and type:

mix test

Mix will compile your project and run all tests defined in the files in the test directory, providing feedback on the success or failure of each one.

Setting up your development environment for TDD in Elixir is a critical step towards developing high-quality software. By following the official installation instructions and using the powerful tools Mix and ExUnit, you'll be well-prepared to adopt TDD practices in your Elixir projects.

WRITING TESTS
WITH EXUNIT

ExUnit is the built-in testing framework in Elixir, designed to be easy to use and extendable. It is enabled by default in every new Elixir project, allowing you to start testing your code immediately.

Unit Tests

Unit tests focus on testing isolated parts of the code, usually individual functions, to ensure they work as expected.

Unit Test Example:

Suppose you have a function that calculates the factorial of a number. First, you would implement the function:

```
my_project > lib > 🔷 math.ex > ...
  1  defmodule Math do
  2    def factorial(0), do: 1
  3    def factorial(n) when n > 0, do: n * factorial(n - 1)
  4  end
  5
```

Then you would write a unit test for this function:

```
my_project > test > 6 math_test.exs > ...
  1   defmodule MathTest do
  2     use ExUnit.Case
  3
  4     test "factorial of 5" do
  5       assert Math.factorial(5) == 120
  6     end
  7   end
  8
```

Integration Tests

Integration tests check how different parts of your system work together. They are particularly useful for ensuring that modules or external services interact correctly with your application.

Integration Test Example:

Imagine you have a system that makes a call to an external API to fetch user information. You could simulate this call in your integration test:

```
my_project > test > 6 user_api_test.exs > ...
  1   defmodule UserApiTest do
  2     use ExUnit.Case
  3
  4     test "fetch user data" do
  5       # API Call Simulation
  6       # Assertion to verify correct integration and data processing
  7     end
  8   end
  9
```

For integration tests, it's common to use mocks or stubs to simulate external parts of the system.

Mock Objects

Mock objects are used to simulate the behavior of real modules in tests, allowing you to test the interaction between modules without relying on external implementations.

In Elixir, using libraries such as Mock, you can create mocks to ensure they behave as expected.

Example of Using Mock with the Mock 0.3 lib:

To install the lib, just configure mix.exs by adding {:mock, "~> 0.3", only: :test} like this:

```
21    # Run "mix help deps" to learn about dependencies.
22    defp deps do
23      [
24        {:mock, "~> 0.3", only: :test}
25      ]
26    end
```

Then run the mix deps.get command to install the new lib.

Next, create the method that will be used with the Mock.

```
my_project > lib > 🔥 my_service.ex > ...
1    defmodule MyService do
2      def fetch_data(term), do: {:ok, term}
3    end
4
```

Now, you can use this mock in your tests to simulate calls to the service:

```
my_project > test > 🔥 my_service_test.exs > ...
1    defmodule MyServiceTest do
2      use ExUnit.Case
3
4      import Mock
5
6      test "uses the mock service" do
7        with_mock(MyService, [fetch_data: fn _ -> {:ok, "mocked response"} end]) do
8          assert MyService.fetch_data(:response) == {:ok, "mocked response"}
9        end
10     end
11   end
12
```

Elixir's ExUnit provides all the necessary tools to write robust unit and integration tests, as well as support for the use of mock objects through external libraries. This approach not only ensures the quality of your code but also promotes better software design, as you think more critically about the interfaces and integrations of your system. With practice and experience, you will become proficient at identifying and writing effective tests for different parts of your system, maximizing the benefits of TDD.

TDD IN ACTION: PRODUCT RATING SYSTEM WITH ELIXIR

Step 1: Defining the Requirement

L et's create a feature that allows adding a rating to a product. Each rating will have a score from 1 to 5.

Step 2: Writing the First Test

We start by writing a test for the add_rating function, which doesn't exist yet. The goal is to add a rating to a product.

test/rating_system_test.exs:

```
my_project > test > ⬦ rating_system_test.exs > ...
 1  defmodule RatingSystemTest do
 2    use ExUnit.Case
 3
 4    test "adds a rating to a product" do
 5      initial_product = %{name: "Tea", ratings: []}
 6      updated_product = RatingSystem.add_rating(initial_product, 5)
 7
 8      assert length(updated_product.ratings) == 1
 9      assert Enum.at(updated_product.ratings, 0) == 5
10    end
11  end
12
```

Step 3: Running the Test

Upon running the test (mix test), it fails because the add_rating function and the RatingSystem module have not been implemented yet. This is the "Red" stage of TDD.

Step 4: Writing Code to Pass the Test

Now, let's implement the function in the simplest way possible to make the test pass.

lib/rating_system.ex:

```
my_project > lib > ⬦ rating_system.ex > ...
 1  defmodule RatingSystem do
 2    def add_rating(product, rating) do
 3      updated_ratings = [rating | product.ratings]
 4      Map.put(product, :ratings, updated_ratings)
 5    end
 6  end
 7
```

Here, we simply add the new rating to the list of existing ratings on the product.

Step 5: Refactoring the Code

The test now passes, but we may want to refactor our code to improve its structure or efficiency.

For example, we might want to ensure that ratings are always stored in order, or we might introduce validation for the rating score.

lib/rating_system.ex (Refactored):

```
my_project > lib > 🔥 rating_system.ex > ...
1   defmodule RatingSystem do
2     def add_rating(product, rating) when rating in 1..5 do
3       updated_ratings = List.insert_at(product.ratings, -1, rating)
4       |> Enum.sort()
5       Map.put(product, :ratings, updated_ratings)
6     end
7   end
8
```

Now, the code not only adds the rating but also ensures that it is within a valid range and keeps the ratings ordered.

Step 6: Reviewing and Continuing Development

After refactoring, run the tests again to ensure that all changes still satisfy the initial requirements. The TDD process is iterative: after completing one cycle, you start the next by writing a new test for the next feature or improvement.

This practical example demonstrates how TDD can be applied in the development of a simple feature in Elixir, starting with a failing test, writing code to pass the test, and finally, refactoring the code to improve quality. The key to TDD is the iterative cycle of testing, which helps build robust and easily maintained software, focusing on the continuous delivery of value through small improvements.

CHAPTER: APPLYING TDD TO A BOOK CRUD WITH PHOENIX

T his chapter will guide you through the development of a CRUD (Create, Read, Update, Delete) application for books, using the Phoenix framework. We will adopt the TDD methodology to implement the listing functionality in our CRUD, and through this, I will share my strategy and approach in project development with TDD. We will implement a database table for books and create tests that cover both the controller and the responsible module, following the principles of TDD.

Installing the Phoenix Framework

To set up Phoenix in your development environment and avoid setbacks during the installation, I recommend visiting the official Phoenix website at https://www.phoenixframework.org and following the detailed instructions to install the latest version of Phoenix.

Starting a Project with Phoenix

To start our project, we will use the command:

mix phx.new app

This command will create a folder named 'app' containing a Phoenix project already configured with the PostgreSQL database. To run the project, you will need to install PostgreSQL or use Docker to run a PostgreSQL database container. I chose the second approach, using the command:

docker run -p 5432:5432 --name db-postgres -e POSTGRES_PASSWORD=postgres -d postgres

With this command, I managed to avoid additional configurations in the Phoenix project. I proceed with the initial commands to build the project:

mix setup

and then:

mix phx.server

After this, accessing the URL localhost:4000 in a browser will allow us to see the home page of the project.

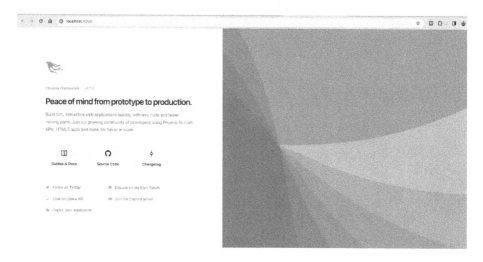

Creating the Book List with TDD

The initial focus will be the development of unit tests, followed by the implementation of the necessary controllers, modules, and database tables to satisfy the tests according to the principles of TDD.

Step 1: Defining the Requirement and creating the test

The initial goal is to test the functionality of listing books. For this, we need an endpoint /books with a GET method that returns the list of books from the database. The test will set these expectations:

app > test > app_web > controllers > 📗 books_controller_test.exs > {} AppWeb.BooksControllerTest

```
 1  defmodule AppWeb.BooksControllerTest do
 2    use AppWeb.ConnCase
 3
 4    describe "index" do
 5      test "returns a list of books", %{conn: conn} do
 6        conn = get(conn, ~p"/books")
 7        assert html_response(conn, 200) =~ "Listing books"
 8        refute html_response(conn, 200) =~ "No books found"
 9      end
10    end
11  end
```

In this test, I expect an HTML return containing a title Listing books and that does not have the phrase No books found to ensure that the test has at least one record in the list.

Step 2: Running the Test

Running the test with (mix test) will not pass, as the implementation has not yet been carried out.

Step 3: Implementing the Necessary Code

We will need an endpoint in the system's routes that responds to the /books route with the GET method, directing to a controller named books_controller.ex, which will initially return an empty list of books in an HTML response.

We will define the endpoint, the controller, the pointer to the template, and the template itself within the controllers/books_html/index.html.heex folder.

```
17    scope "/", AppWeb do
18      pipe_through :browser
19
20      get "/", PageController, :home
21      get "/books", BooksController, :index
22    end
23
```

We'll create the controller like this:

app > lib > app_web > controllers > 🌢 books_controller.ex > ...

```
1   defmodule AppWeb.BooksController do
2     use AppWeb, :controller
3
4     def index(conn, _params) do
5       books = []
6       render(conn, :index, books: books)
7     end
8   end
9
```

Point to our template:

app > lib > app_web > controllers > 🌢 books_html.ex > ...

```
1   defmodule AppWeb.BooksHTML do
2     use AppWeb, :html
3
4     embed_templates "books_html/*"
5   end
6
```

And create the template inside the controllers/books_html/ index.html.heex folder:

app > lib > app_web > controllers > books_html > ≡ index.html.heex

```
1   <h1>Listing books</h1>
2   <%= if Enum.empty?(@books) do %>
3     <p>No books found</p>
4   <% else %>
5     <%= for book <- @books do %>
6       <div class="book">
7         <h2 class="title-book"><%= book.title %></h2>
8         <p><%= book.author %></p>
9         <p><%= book.description %></p>
10      </div>
11    <% end %>
12  <% end %>
13
```

With all this, the test will still show an error because we still do not have any books created in the database, and the error that will appear when running the test will be related to the assert:

refute html_response(conn, 200) =~ "No books found"

Since our test is still red, we need to continue implementing what is missing until the test turns green. But here at this point, we will have an important detail. What is missing now is a module that will access the database and list the books, and when we move from control-level tests, we need to create another test that will cover the application's module level. So let's create this new unit test called books_test.ex and it will be inside the test/app/books_test.exs folder:

```
app > test > app > 📓 books_test.exs > ...
  1  defmodule AppWeb.BooksTest do
  2    use App.DataCase
  3
  4    describe "list_all/0" do
  5      test "returns a list of books" do
  6        books = App.Books.list_all()
  7
  8        assert Enum.count(books) != 0
  9      end
 10    end
 11  end
 12
```

At this point, note that when running the tests, we will have 2 failures, and the new failure indicates that the module and method Books.list_all() do not exist. We need to continue creating the modules and methods to resolve this error, and following this way, we will end up realizing that we need to create a table in the database and then create the listing of the records. Let's start by creating a migration that will be responsible for creating a table in the database using the command:

mix ecto.gen.migration create_books_table

And define the migration:

app > priv > repo > migrations > 🔖 20240214165147_create_books_table.exs > ...

```
1  defmodule App.Repo.Migrations.CreateBooksTable do
2    use Ecto.Migration
3
4    def change do
5      create table(:books) do
6        add :title, :string
7        add :author, :string
8        add :description, :string
9
10        timestamps()
11      end
12    end
13  end
14
```

And then run the command:

mix ecto.migrate

The next step is to create the Schema that will represent this book table within the system. We will define it in the file:

app/lib/app/book/book.ex

```
app > lib > app > book >  book.ex > ...
   1  defmodule App.Book do
   2    use Ecto.Schema
   3    import Ecto.Changeset
   4
   5    schema "books" do
   6      field :title, :string
   7      field :author, :string
   8      field :description, :string
   9
  10      timestamps()
  11    end
  12
  13    @doc false
  14    def changeset(book, attrs) do
  15      book
  16      |> cast(attrs, [:title, :author, :description])
  17      |> validate_required([:title, :author, :description])
  18    end
  19  end
  20
```

We still need to define the module to list the books in app/book/books.ex

```
app > lib > app > book >  books.ex > ...
   1  defmodule App.Books do
   2    alias App.Book
   3    alias App.Repo
   4
   5    def list_all() do
   6      Repo.all(Book)
   7    end
   8  end
   9
```

At this moment, our tests are almost passing. What is missing is to create book records to use in our tests, and for that, we will create a BooksFixtures to insert books into the database in our tests:

```
app > test > support > fixtures > 🔥 books_fixtures.ex > ...
 1   defmodule App.BooksFixtures do
 2
 3     alias App.Book
 4     alias App.Repo
 5
 6     def books_fixture(attrs \\ %{}) do
 7       %Book{
 8         title: "The Pragmatic Programmer",
 9         author: "Andrew Hunt and David Thomas",
10         description: "The Pragmatic Programmer ..."
11       }
12       |> Book.changeset(attrs)
13       |> Repo.insert!()
14     end
15   end
16
```

And then we will run this BooksFixtures in the Module tests:

```
app > test > app > 🔥 books_test.exs > ...
 1   defmodule App.BooksTest do
 2     use App.DataCase
 3
 4     import App.BooksFixtures
 5
 6     describe "list_all/0" do
 7       test "returns a list of books" do
 8         books_fixture()
 9         books = App.Books.list_all()
10
11         assert Enum.count(books) != 0
12       end
13     end
14   end
15
```

And in the control tests:

```
app > test > app_web > controllers > 📗 books_controller_test.exs > …
 1  defmodule AppWeb.BooksControllerTest do
 2    use AppWeb.ConnCase
 3
 4    import App.BooksFixtures
 5
 6    describe "index" do
 7      test "returns a list of books", %{conn: conn} do
 8        books_fixture()
 9        conn = get(conn, ~p"/books")
10        assert html_response(conn, 200) =~ "Listing books"
11        refute html_response(conn, 200) =~ "No books found"
12      end
13    end
14  end
15
```

With this, we will run the tests again to finally arrive at the green color informing that all requirements have been met.

Step 4: Refactoring and Evolving

At this stage, we have the opportunity to further refine the user interface, introducing advanced functionalities such as filters or sorting options. This will involve adapting the existing tests and refactoring the code to accommodate these new features. The TDD process allows us to make these improvements safely and efficiently, ensuring that any new functionality is well tested and integrated without disruptions.

This step-by-step method is fundamental for the progressive development of a robust application. By following this approach, we ensure a high-quality final delivery, free of defects, and with complete coverage of business rules, providing confidence to both the development team and stakeholders.

COMMON CHALLENGES WHEN ADOPTING TDD AND HOW TO OVERCOME THEM

Challenge 1: Cultural Resistance

Problem

Often, teams may resist adopting TDD because they are not familiar with the benefits it can bring or believe it will slow down development.

Solution

Education and Training: Offer workshops and training sessions to show the benefits of TDD.

Demonstration by Results: Start with a pilot project to demonstrate how TDD can improve code quality and reduce bugs.

Challenge 2: Difficulty in Writing Tests Before Code

Problem

Writing tests before code can be counter-intuitive for those accustomed to writing code first and testing afterward.

Solution

Practice and Patience: Encourage constant practice of TDD to develop a test-first mindset.

Mentorship and Pair Programming: Use pair programming with a TDD-experienced member to guide those less experienced.

Challenge 3: Keeping Tests Relevant

Problem

As the project grows, old tests may become irrelevant or redundant, leading to a bloated and difficult-to-maintain test base.

Solution

Regular Test Review: Incorporate test review as part of the refactoring process to remove or update obsolete tests.

Focus on Test Documentation: Document the purpose of each test to facilitate future maintenance.

Challenge 4: Dealing with Fragile Tests

Problem

Tests that rely too much on the system state or specific

configurations can become fragile and break frequently, even with minimal changes in code.

Solution

Use Mocks and Stubs: Isolate test components using mocks and stubs to reduce dependencies.
Test Behaviors, Not Implementations: Focus on testing what the code should do, not how it does it.

Challenge 5: Slow Tests

Problem:

A large test suite can become very slow, discouraging its frequent execution.

Solution

Test Suite Optimization: Identify and optimize the slowest tests. For instance, reduce database access or external resources.

Parallel Test Execution: Utilize parallel test execution features available in many frameworks to speed up execution.

Adopting TDD is a long-term commitment that can face initial resistance and practical challenges. However, by proactively addressing these challenges and maintaining an open mindset for learning and adaptation, teams can reap significant benefits of TDD, including higher code quality, reduced bugs, and a more sustainable codebase. Remember, the key to success with TDD is constant practice, review, and optimization of tests to ensure they remain relevant and efficient.

ACKNOWLEDGEMENT

As this journey comes to its end, I would like to take a moment to express my deep gratitude to all those who made this book possible. Writing about Test-Driven Development (TDD) in practice with Elixir has been both a challenging and rewarding experience, and it would not have been the same without the support and encouragement from many.

First and foremost, my eternal gratitude goes to my family. To my wife, Aline, for her infinite patience, love, and constant encouragement, even during the most tumultuous times of the writing process. To my son, Murilo, for being a continual source of inspiration and joy. You are my safe harbor and the reason I strive to be better every day.

To my parents, sister, and all my extended family, thank you for believing in me and supporting me unconditionally in all my endeavors. Your unwavering faith in my potential has been one of my greatest motivators.

A special thank you to my friends, who provided listening ears and wise advice when I needed it most. Your companionship and support were crucial in keeping my spirits and focus.

To my colleagues and tech leads, whose unique perspectives, shared experience, and collaborative support have greatly enriched my understanding and application of TDD. Working alongside you has been a constant source of learning and inspiration.

I cannot fail to express my gratitude to the thousands of students I have had the pleasure of teaching over the years. Your enthusiasm for learning, thought-provoking questions, and ongoing dedication have been a constant reminder of why I chose this path. This book is also for you, in the hope that it serves as a valuable tool on your learning journey.

Last but certainly not least, I am thankful to the Elixir community for its welcoming, collaborative, and innovative spirit. Without the hard work and passion of everyone contributing to this community, this book would not be possible.

This book is the culmination of many hours of work, learning, and collaboration. Every word written is a testament to the support and encouragement I have received along this path. To all of you, my most sincere thanks.

ABOUT THE AUTHOR

Guilherme Ferreira

Guilherme graduated in Computer Science
from the University of Santa Cruz do Sul
(UNISC), where he began his journey into
the vast world of technology. He currently
works as a Software Engineer and holds the
position of Tech Lead, demonstrating not
only his technical competence but also his
ability to lead teams in developing
innovative solutions.

With a deep passion for sharing knowledge, Guilherme has
dedicated himself to teaching various courses on the Udemy
platform. His courses cover a wide range of topics in the
field of software engineering, including but not limited to,
agile development, Test-Driven Development (TDD) practices,
and programming in Elixir. Through his practical and didactic
approach, he has helped students and professionals around the
world to enhance their skills and better understand the principles
governing the development of high-quality software.

Guilherme's decision to write a book on TDD with Elixir stems
from his desire to consolidate his knowledge and experience into
a comprehensive resource that can serve both beginners and
experienced developers. He firmly believes that TDD is not just a
development methodology but a philosophy that can transform
the way we think and create software, making the process more

efficient, reliable, and, above all, rewarding.

Guilherme continues to explore new technologies and methodologies, always looking for ways to improve software quality and the effectiveness of development teams. He hopes that by sharing his experiences and insights through this book, he can inspire others to follow a similar path of continuous learning and innovation.